Maybe Today

Maybe Today

Poems by Barry Dickson

Cherry Grove Collections

Published by Cherry Grove Collections
P.O. Box 541106
Cincinnati, OH 45254-1106

ISBN: 9781625493743

Poetry Editor: Kevin Walzer
Business Editor: Lori Jareo

Visit us on the web at www.cherry-grove.com

ACKNOWLEDGEMENTS

North American Review: "Barry Dickson 1945–"

Pearl Literary Magazine: "The Adverbial World of Match.com"

Heeltap: "Dear Citibank"

Haiku Journal: (haiku #4)

HazMat Literary Review: "Family Values"

Reflections: "Message from My Late Mother to All Governments"

Ebb and Flow: "Prescription"

asininepoetry.com: "Honk"

Genie: "Thank God for Gravity"

Reflections: Mane-Man and Toughie

Ebb and Flow: "Yet Another If-I-Had-Life-To-Do-All-Over-Again Poem"

Gratitude to everyone at The Frost Place, Palm Beach Poetry Festival and Island Writers' Network.

Thank you, Eric Nelson, Joan Houlihan, Andrew Clark, Elizabeth Robin, Sheryl DelGigante, Kathy Bradford and Miho Kinnas for your manuscript feedback.

Cover design: Wayne Schombs

for Kathy, Sheryl
and all who were encouraging

Table of Contents

The Adverbial World Of Match.Com

Your profile says that you are quite.

It also states you can be very. Sometimes even very very.

In addition, I see that you are partly and slightly,

not to mention mostly, though you did mention it nine times.

Thanks for writing, but I'm looking

for someone who's extremely.

I also have a soft spot in my heart for highly,

but there I'll try to compromise.

One place, however, I will not bend.

You mention several times you never.

Forgive me, please, I'd like someone

who at least occasionally.

And frankly, even at my age,

I wouldn't mind a mate who often.

Yet Another If-I-Had-Life-To-Do-All-Over-Again Poem

First, I would shut up more.
I discovered one cannot talk and learn at the same time.
Oddly, I *could* talk and listen. But it would always be me
I'm listening to. And never once, in all my life,
did I ever hear myself say something I didn't already know.

This time I will not leave the hospital early the day my mother dies,
just because I'm feeling fidgety. I will be there when she goes,
to say good-bye to someone who thought
all my ideas brilliant, all my jokes hilarious
and "Warren Beatty and Brad Pitt could only wish they had such a face."
Most of us don't get more than one of those in a lifetime.

Speaking of which, this time I will not let Lucinda Gluck go,
just because I thought her ultimatum was "too soon."
Too soon for what, Barry? Too soon to be loved?
Too soon to have a best friend for life?
Too soon to go to bed every night with the smartest, most
beautiful woman in eastern Pennsylvania?
Clearly it wasn't too soon to be an asshole.
And if she ever reads this, I will be mortified.

That's another thing I will do this time around: Be mortified more.
This business of not doing because of what might happen
creates a life lived in place. Before life can go somewhere good,
it must first simply go. Like Yogi said,
"We're lost, but we're makin' good time."

Message From My Late Mother To All Governments

In Loving Memory: Lillian Davis Dickson Siswein

Here here, no fighting. Stop it!

Be careful with that, you'll hurt someone.

All right you guys, knock it off.

Eh, eh, no hitting, no hitting...I don't care

who started it, no hitting.

Don't leave this place looking like a cyclone hit it.

What in the world is going on?

Now look what you've done.

Dear Citibank,

Thank you for the warning that this was my "Last Chance!" to take advantage of your 0% credit card offer. Thank you for the mailing a month later also marked on the envelope "Last Chance!" And for the one six weeks after that, again labeled "Last Chance!" Thank you, especially, for the two last chances that followed that one the next week. Five last chances! If only we all had such patience in our human intercourse.

But wait, there's more!

When my sixth last chance arrived this morning, I could hardly contain myself. Is there no limit to your indulgence? Is hoping there's yet another last chance en route asking too much? I truly hope my most recent last chance was not my last last chance, something I have dreaded ever since my first last chance.

Looking forward hopefully to my next last chance,

Barry Dickson

Everywhere

"Where are you going, dear?" she called from upstairs.
"Out looking for a poem. I'll be back at dinnertime. Bye."

I will find one in the park for sure.
It might land on a branch.
Or bend my way in a breeze.
Or poke its little head up through the ground.
Once I found a poem in the park pond
making tiny bubbles with its lips.
Look, I said to my friend Freddie, a poem.
"What are you talking about," he said,
"it's a damn fish." Good guy, that Freddie;
not so good at seeing poems.

If I don't find one in the park
I'll be surprised, but not discouraged.
There are plenty on the streets—
under cars, in skimpy skirts,
they even sleep in doorways.
Arnold once found a beauty on a beach.
Whitman on a little promontory.
Keats on an urn. Byron in darkness.
Wow, an eye so sharp

you could spot a poem in the dark.

Most poems are dying to be found.
They call to you from everywhere.
Train wheels. Bell peals. Pounding hearts.
Frost found several in the snow.
(A guy named Frost finding poems in the snow
is in itself a little poem, don't you think?)
Byron even heard one call from inside Anne
not to mention Florence, Harriet, Caroline, Marion and Mary.
Apparently it's true, women love a man who listens.

So what then is the population of these poems,
there being no census for such things?
Some say they are countless billions. A poem in every
flake and bird and kiss and blade
and branch and wing and rose and nose and leaf
and child and flea and field and tear and soul and heart.

But there is yet another school, calling poems extremely rare.
You must search long and wander miles for weeks or
months to find just one, they say. And even then
they often are imposters, like fool's gold.
They claim there have been maybe a few thousand ever, tops.
Tough crowd.

I favor the former. But perhaps the latter have a point
because I found no poem that day—how odd.
Last week, I found one in the glove compartment.
I don't know how long it had been in there,
or why I never noticed it before—between the unpaid parking tickets,
the expired insurance card, and the empty space
where the registration should have been.
I called it *Negligence: An Ode.*

That evening, as promised, I did return at dinnertime.
We went to Jean Jacque's Bistro, our favorite local spot,
where I had my favorite local soup.
But tonight…I noticed something I had never seen before.
One crouton, a large grayish one, seemed to wander aimlessly,
as though rudderless. Whilst a smaller one floated
directly for it, I suspect deliberately.
The big one, I thought, it's the Bismarck.
The small one, H.M.S. Hood. I gasped.
"What's the matter?" said my girlfriend.
I turned to the kitchen and called out:
"Waiter! There's a poem in my soup!"

Ode To Snow

It used to be a bicycle,
now it's a Harley.
It was a pitchfork, now a
dachshund with three tails.
See that face over there
with the fat lips?
My barbecue grill
has become Mick Jagger.
And when did the Smiths
move into a cathedral,
their chimney becoming
a steeple? Showoffs!
Oh snow! Make my little shack
a Colonial mansion
(before your weight makes it a pancake).
And that lamppost, snow?
Turn it into a lovely, shapely woman,
someone to get me through
the long, lonely winter,
—my heart now as empty as my nest—
who listens when I need to share,
who whistles at me on windy nights.
I will open up to her and love her,

even though I know
she will leave me in the spring.

The Refrigerator-Light Controversy: Solved

It goes out.
I know this for sure because as a child
I got stuck in there. Slam!
Trust me, it goes out.
By the way, it's not just Slam! It's Brrrr!, too.
I can report to you, also, it goes back on
when your mother opens the door
to get some jelly
and there's her son in a jam,
curled up next to the nectarines,
like this year the holiday turkey
is wearing little Reeboks.
She screams. Then begins to tremble.
Imagine, I'm the one stuck in the cold
but *she* trembles.
Boy, it's all about you, huh, mom?

Next week: The Chicken-Egg Controversy: Solved.

Faux Real

I would not dare buy a real fur
for this lovely, liberal lover of the furry.
So in I went to Feinstein's Furs
for the best faux fur real money could buy.
"Nineteen hundred sixty-six," Fanny Feinstein quoted.
"For a *faux fur*?" I asked.
"There's this one over here for 799," she replied.
"Looks just as good to me,
what would be the difference?"
"This one," said Fanny, "is not a real faux fur."
"Gimme the best you got. Gimme the real fake thing."

Lucinda was delighted with the faux fur that I bought her.
She stripped, and put on her faux fur.
As we made love, I did my usual yelling
though slightly muffled through faux fur.
Lucinda seemed to scream a little, too.
Afterward, I couldn't help but wonder.
"Was that orgasm real?" I asked. She looked defensive.
"Have you ever faked one?" I persisted.
She paused. "Well, *you* know there was the night
we discussed if you could tell."
"Yes," I said. "You claimed you had just faked one and that I didn't
know.

But I thought you didn't really fake it, you were just saying so."
"But why would I fake faking it?" she asked me from her faux.

The next thing that we always do is turn on the TV.
And there they were, the Presidential candidates.
"You know," I said, "it strikes me that they are saying
what they think we want to hear."
"Yes," replied Lucinda. "but sometimes
they really do believe what they are saying."
"You mean that they are faking their sincerity
but sometimes they mean it when they fake?" I asked
snuggling up to her and her faux fur.

I finally had enough faux faking for one day and fell asleep.
Soon I began to dream.
Now, dreams by definition are all fake.
You're not really flying. Your teeth aren't really falling out.

But, you see, dreams never are faux fake.
They put on their little show and go away when you awake.
They don't hang around to overcharge you.
Or manipulate your vote. Or trick you with their lust.
Dreams are what this world needs more of:
A faker you can trust.

Birds Of A Feather

Tiny sparrows come begging
for crumbs from my morning sandwich—
what a way to make a living.

Yet soon, inside, we will light
on our chairs, competing for bread,
scouring the halls for morsels of approval,
tilting our heads at little angles
to listen for hints on what to say next,
inching toward telling the truth
then flying away at the first sign of danger.

People Don't Want Drills, They Want Holes

People don't want holes, they want shelves.
People don't want shelves, they want a place to display
expensive knickknacks.
People don't want a place to display expensive knickknacks,
they want compliments.

People don't want drills, they want love.

Thank God For Gravity

It keeps me here on earth.
Otherwise I would fly off into space.
Then what would I do? I have no friends out there.
They say the Venusians are a friendly, welcoming people.
But it's not easy breaking into a group
that has pre-existing social bonds.
Especially when they have more arms
and eyes and heads than you.
And at my age,
I could do without others gawking,
saying things like, "Don't turn around,
but guess who just walked in—
that guy with no antennae."

Besides, who wants to live where there's not
·a single good sushi place within a billion miles.
Come to think of it, maybe that's a business opportunity—
a guy's gotta make a living even on Corona Borealis.
Though I wonder: Would you eat fish that's
been traveling for 40 light years?
How about I open a standup club.
"Welcome to Andromedy Comedy.
Ladies and gentlemen, put your
prehensile tentacles together for…"

No, I think I like it right here.
We have the loveliest flowers
of nearly any planet anywhere.
Despite what they say, there's still
plenty of fresh air around.
And I wouldn't want to live
if I could never hear again
the most beautiful sound in the universe:
A woman laughing.

Pillow Talk

I have not changed pillow cases since you left
six weeks ago, just to keep your scent around.
Each morning I wake up spooning a quilt
rolled into a Lucinda surrogate.

Remember, every night I would call you Toasty
and you would call me Roasty
and we pledged never to reveal these embarrassments
though you feared one day they would show up in a poem,
but I reassured you?

Remember how we would whisper when the lights went out
until it occurred to us, there's no one else here
what the heck are we always whispering for?

Remember the night you woke me at 3AM just to make love
and we did and the next morning I had no recollection of it?
Boy were you pissed. (Incidentally, if *You're beautiful
when you're angry* is so patronizing, why did your
teal blue eyes smile every time I said it?)

Remember the night I told you
you're the smart funny one,
and you kept saying, *no you're the smart funny one.*

And finally I said *OK, I'm the smart, funny one* and you said
What the hell is that supposed to mean?

Remember how I would fake snoring?
The truth can now be told.
I was only faking half the time.

Remember the night I laughed so hard
I fell out of bed and you wouldn't let me back in
and I said *OK then, I'll just get in my car*
and go stay in a luxury hotel somewhere
and I did, and you got in your car and followed me
and we spent that amazing night at the Plaza?

You know, when I returned from shopping Sunday
my friend Jack, the shrink, said he thinks I'm finally
getting over you. I asked how he knew and he said
look in the bag. And there they were.
New pillow cases.

I guess he didn't notice they were teal blue.

Honk

Honk if you love Jesus.
Honk if you love Buddha.
Honk if you love me.
Honk if you'd rather be fishing. I'll honk back if I'd also
rather you be fishing
'cause I've seen how you drive.

Honk if you're hopeful.
Honk if you're horny.
Honk if you're a honky.
Honk if you're a goose, not that you'd have many options.
Honk if you're a goose who is politically, esthetically and morally
opposed to foie gras.

Honk if you hate like holy hell hokey alliteration,
especially when it's heavy-handed.
Honk if you'll marry me right now.
Honk if you love Trump/Pence.
Honk if you're having second thoughts about that last honk.
But most of all, please, we'd all love to see you
honk if your horn is broken.

He's Right

"That six million number is pure bullshit."

Carl E., holocaust denier, at neo-Nazi rally

When you kill a child, you kill his children too,
and the children of their children.
They say six million died,
but by now it must be 25, soon it will be 30.
When you kill a child, the killing
never ever ever stops.

Open Poem To A Snob

When the voice of NASA said, "The LEM
has lifted from the moon, our men
are now returning home," his timing was a little off.
They were returning home when they lifted from the earth.
Scientists are now quite sure that we are all from outer space,
amino acids landing here bubbling in primordial ooze.
Please do not tell me you originate from Greenwich,
summer in Newport
and winter in Palm Springs.
Like me, you hail from Betelgeuse,
Andromeda, Orion's buckle.
(Though you are quite white, who knows,
you may have once been green.)
When the Bible says we are from dust and
unto dust we shall return, that isn't dust of Earth,
but dust of space.
You might be relieved to know
that you are full of something other than yourself.
Like me, you are full of stardust.

So do not think you are hot stuff,
you are only *from* hot stuff.
And you didn't get here by fancy car.

As with all of us,
you arrived by comet.

(haiku #4)

The woods beckon me,
come in, look around, enjoy.
No exit assured.

Wild Fling

I called that night to set up our blind date,
to tell you this is Murray, Marcy's friend.
When your machine picked up I thought, my goodness
what a lovely voice, thank you, Marcy,
so far this is going quite well.
You said *Hi, this is Adrianna, thanks so much for calling*.
So polite, I thought, so sweet.
I could already feel us growing closer.
See! It doesn't take so much to please me—
all this talk that I'm too picky, Mr. Bachelor here
looking for excuses not to get involved. Commitmentphobe my ass.
When you went on to say *I hope that you're enjoying this great day,*
my heart began to palpitate.
Someone who thinks of others' feelings!
I know it sounds so crazy, I know the pacing's off,
but was I really starting to feel love?

That's when it happened. On a certain level I felt it coming.
I knew that you were too good to be true.
That you would find a way to sabotage the closeness. It never fails.
I'm not here right now, you said. Oh really? How can that be?
You were there when you recorded that; yet you said *I'm not here*.
Adrianna, how can someone not be where they are?
If there is one thing I can't stand in a relationship it's lying.

Leave a message please, I promise I'll get back to you real soon.
Yeah, like I'm supposed to trust you now?

Needless to say, I did not leave a message.
Once you've betrayed me, I will never speak to you again.
You can cry your way through an entire box of tissues.
But you'll never get back Murray Marcy's friend.
'Cause clearly, Adrianna, you've got issues.

Prescription

Feeling a pain deep inside,
or occasional emptiness?
Consider taking poetry.

(Those who are pregnant or could become pregnant
should read poetry with caution. Poetry can cause
you to do things that might make you pregnant.
Poetry can alter the shape of your heart.
In some cases, successfully publishing poetry has caused swelling of the head.
Poetry makes people see things that aren't really there.
It can cause drowsiness, and reactions to certain poetry
have been misdiagnosed as narcolepsy.
Poetry has been linked to mood swings—weeping to fits of laughter.
Do not mix poetry with alcohol, the poet has taken care of that.
Certain people have severe reactions to poetry. In critics, for example,
it can provoke nastiness and impaired judgment.
Cases of Tourette's have been reported, readers blurting out "Huh?"
or "What the hell does that mean?"
If poetry results in an erection lasting more than four hours,
consult a hot English teacher.)

Ask your doctor if poetry is right for you!

Maybe Today

for David Rodriguez Ritcheson
(At a Texas BBQ, a 16-year-old Mexican-American was beaten
nearly to death by 2 white boys for talking to their sister. A year later,
after testifying before Congress on hate crimes, he committed suicide.)

The sun descends, offended by earth.
Or is it earth, embarrassed, turns away?
Whichever, soon the great optimist, morning,
will give it yet another try.
Maybe today will be the day
no one is dragged behind a truck
because he's black
or kicked to death because he's gay,
the day no man imprisons a girl,
no mother drowns a child.
Maybe today will be the day the cycle ends—
where one man builds a building
and another man flies a plane into it.
I tell morning: *They say*
doing the same thing
expecting different results
defines insanity.
Morning answers: *Maybe it*
defines optimism. Maybe today.

Delicious

You guaranteed victory.
Talked even landslide.
You told me his stand
on civil liberties will
sweep him in,
that I have "no
feel for these things"
but you have your
"finger on the pulse
of the people."
I argued the pulse,
but gave you the finger.

He lost.

And now, *my* stand
on civil liberties:
Freedom of speech
is like food.
I may not agree
with your words,
but I will fight to
the death for your
right to eat them.

Mane-Man and Toughie

for Sheryl, Kathy, Colleen, and all people who love animals.

"...I do not hunt and hope you do not, too.
You kill Bambi, I might have to kill you."
            email from Barb323 *on Match.com*

On a farm in a part of the country that need not be named
——this is a story about friendship and friendship is everywhere—
there lived a horse, Mane Man, and a cat, Toughie.
When Toughie one day showed up in the doorway of the barn
both just froze, in a cross-species stare.
Neither moving for at least a minute.
(But don't a lot of friendships begin with caution,
and sometimes they're the ones that last?)
From that day on they were never seen apart
not once for 14 years.
Playing, running, sleeping, and, one witness claims, even joking.
They ate together.
Mane-Man always leaving just a little oats
in the bottom of the bag—something he
never did pre-Toughie.
Toughie would have no part of oats of course,
being mainly a connoisseur of fish.
But fair is fair. Mane-Man never once

touched a morsel of the mouse
Toughie would on occasion bring him.
They slept together.
Farmer Edson—and sometimes Mrs. Edson—loved
to watch them share the stall.
"You think you've seen it all," he told his neighbor, "when you find
your cat spooning your horse. Until one morning
you see your half-ton horse spooning your nine-pound cat."
Everyday they ran together back and forth across the field,
from the maple round the poplar then back again to maple.
They would always rest in the maple's shade,
Mane-Man's wispy tail more concerned
with flicking flies from Toughie than from himself.

Then, there was the night of the coyote
flashing fangs in the doorway of the barn.
Toughie hid up in the loft behind a bail.

That is, until coyote began to creep toward
the tethered horse, neighing, terrified and wide-eyed.
That's when Toughie leaped down from the loft
snarling, hissing, clawing, biting.
Farmer Edson saw the beast two times since that night.
He has now dubbed him Wile-E One-Eye.

Every month, Farmer Edson had his hoe-down.

Folks would gather on his lawn
from every corner of the county,
sometimes even from beyond.
And he would play that fiddle.
Oh, how he loved to play that fiddle.
They all would clap and stomp
and swing their partners round and round.
In 40 years with this easy, humble man
Mrs. Edson only saw him angry twice.
Once when she nearly sat on the fiddle,
once when she nearly sat on the bow.

No one knows if it's to be believed
but Jenny Winston, Sheriff Winston's teenage kid,
says that one night during the hoe-down
she wandered to the barn
to get away from all the smoke and noise
(but you could hear the fiddle still)
when she came running back and made the claim.
"They're dancing!" she said. "The horse and cat
were moving to the music!
The cat was running round the horse
and the horse was stamping hooves!"
"You've gone whack-a-ding-hoy," old Martha Johnston said.
"No, I tell you they were dancing!"
Who knows if it is true?

One autumn night, lo and behold,
there it was, a horse's nose
gently thumping on the kitchen pane.
"How did he get loose?!" Mrs. Edson asked
They followed Mane-Man to the barn
and found Toughie looking not so tough.
Choking, gagging, struggling to breathe.
They rushed him to Doc Walkoff.
Thankfully, Toughie only had to stay a couple nights.

But in that time Mane Man did not eat
and on the second night Farmer Edson found him
in the barn on his boney horse's knees.
"Tellin' nobody about this one," he said.
"They didn't believe the spooning or the dancing.
They sure ain't gonna believe the praying."

The years carried on, as did the playing and the running
and the joking and the resting and the sharing
and the spooning and the dancing and the flicking.
One hot afternoon after they were running round
Farmer Edson felt a thump come through the ground.
He ran over to the maple and there
was Mane Man--no flicking, no movement, no breath.
He knew what had happened right away.
And right away he knew what would be coming next.

Toughie held out about three days,
refusing all the while to ever leave that maple
right until the very end.

On a night not so long thereafter, Mrs. Edson was awakened
by a sound coming from the grave sites underneath the maple.
Was that digging?
When farmer Edson came back to the bed
she knew she should not ask.
Somehow she also knew she should not
ask about his extra trips to town
that came right after that.

Some weeks later it was time
for yet another hoe-down.
Once again they all gathered on the lawn
and once again they all clapped and stomped.
But tonight, there was a special look
On Farmer Edson's face.
And, oh, the extra sweetness, even joy,
in the music that he played
as he stood in front of all his friends
dancing to the rhythm of his bow—
with its brand new horse hairs, and his fiddle
with its shiny, fresh gut strings.

Mane Man and Toughie playing together yet again.
This time, forever and ever.

Family Values

That's him you hear up there somewhere
calling for a mate to start a brood.
The white-breasted sapsucker.

She taps and taps all day for mites
to feed her hatchlings lunch.
The red-crested woodpecker.

He sends another's chicks to die
but wouldn't go himself.
The yellow-bellied cocksucker.

At The 92nd St. Y

The college kid approaches the mike
and asks the Poet Laureate.
"Sir, when you write humorous verse,
don't you do so at the risk of sacrificing depth?"
But what could be deeper than humor?
Does a belly laugh come from a
shallower place than a tear?

Silence

I am amazed at how quiet the stars are.
Not a peep.
You would think a 400-billion-ton ball of burning gas
hurtling 64 million miles a minute
would at least make a swooshing sound.
I mean, the people upstairs can't even
flush a toilet without waking me up.
I know, I know, sound does not travel through space
because it is a vacuum and therefore there is
no medium to carry it.
But don't give me that. I saw *Star Wars*.
You can hear a laser beam hit a space ship
across this vacuum, BOOM!
Apparently, we need sound so much
we put it where it's not.

So how come we're not better listeners?

Barry Dickson 1945–

The instant you are born, you get a dash.

A reminder the day life begins that one day it will end. Guaranteed.

Joe Jones, 1966 dash. Jennifer Kristin Rabinowitz, 2021 dash.

Somewhere in a county seat, a very willing clerk

sits ready to write a year to the right of your dash.

Michael Jackson, 1958 dash 2009.

You cannot have your dash removed…there are no dashectomies.

You cannot get rid of your dash by living a good life. Sorry.

One man does not have a bigger dash than another man.

Rich people cannot cheat death by buying more dashes; Bill Gates'

dash is identical to the dash of the bag lady

you passed on your way to work this morning.

Nothing personal, but your dash is worthless.

You cannot sell it for one penny or auction it on eBay.

Are you a Christian? You cannot be saved from the dash.

A Jew? 5800 years of history have not removed one single dash.

A Muslim? All the passion and intensity on earth will never delete
your dash.

A Buddhist? You have gained great wisdom. Guess what. You still
have a dash.

So as long as there is an empty space to the right of your dash, enjoy.
Live, love, learn. And be nice to that other guy.
Because no matter who he is or what he's done,
no matter who you are or who you think you are,
I can assure you, with absolute certainty, that you both have a dash
and a very willing county clerk.

Printed in Great Britain
by Amazon

65645296R00033